BASIC READING SERIES

WORKBOOK

LEVEL E

Kittens and Children

by Donald Rasmussen and Lynn Goldberg

BASIC READING
BERKELEY·CALIFORNIA

To Parents and Teachers

Donald Rasmussen and Lynn Goldberg developed the BASIC READING SERIES (BRS) in the early 1960s at the Miquon School, a small parent-teacher cooperative near Philadelphia. At that time, most children were taught to read using the "sight" or "look-say" method epitomized by the "Dick and Jane" readers, and many were left behind. Don and Lynn knew there must be a better way, so they spent five years developing their own reading program based on the work of the renowned linguist Leonard Bloomfield. They called their method *"inductive whole-word phonics, with a strong linguistics research base."*

After tryouts in inner-city and suburban schools around the country and almost a dozen revisions, the BASIC READING SERIES was published by Science Research Associates (SRA) and enjoyed great success. Over the years, other reading methods have come and then gone out of favor. Now, decades later, phonics is recognized as the scientific approach to reading instruction, and the BASIC READING SERIES is once again available.

BRS is divided into six levels — Levels A to F — with a reader and a workbook for each level. In Level E, children are introduced to longer words representing five or more distinct sounds as well as multisyllabic words, usually words in which the first syllable is stressed and the final syllable is a common suffix, such as *asked*, *batter*, or *flatten*. Also introduced are words with vowel digraphs, such as *beet* and *rain*; words with diphthongs, such as *boil* and *lawn*; the five "long" vowels; inflected endings; and multisyllabic words with unstressed first or last syllables.

The BRS Workbooks

The workbooks for BRS contain material with which children can practice their decoding skills independently of teacher direction. The decoding experiences thus provided increase the children's opportunities to discover sound-spelling relationships and to develop automatic word recognition. The workbooks are also an aid to vocabulary, word-meaning, and concept development, as they lead children to associate words with appropriate visual images and challenge children to deal with the meanings of words, phrases, and sentences. Finally, the workbooks are a useful tool with which to evaluate the children's decoding progress.

The workbook for Level E has nine sections of exercises, which correspond (in their sound-spelling patterns only) to the nine sections of the Level E reader, *Kittens and Children*. The exercises are not tied to the story content of the reader, however. Each section is identified by numbered tabs in the margins of its pages and begins with word charts that present the new words for that section of Level E. Each section progresses from simple exercises based on single words and phrases to more complex exercises involving sentences and short stories.

The workbook is easy to use. Children answer each item in one of three ways: by circling a word or phrase; by writing a numeral in a box; or by placing an X in a circle. Since no handwriting skill is needed, the children's reading progress is kept independent of their handwriting progress. The reading lesson can proceed regardless of the children's handwriting abilities.

Some suggestions for the most effective use of the Level E workbook:

1. Do not ask the children to do the work in a given section of the workbook until they have become acquainted with the sound-spelling patterns used in that section. You may want to begin each section of the workbook by reading the word charts for that section with the children. Have the children read up and down the columns, and discuss any unfamiliar words with them before proceeding to the exercises.

2. Throughout the first section of Level E, take care to see that each child understands the directions and is following them correctly before encouraging them to proceed on their own

3. If a child does not recognize a pictured object, simply tell them what it is.

4. Whenever possible, correct the children's work with them, reading the words, phrases, and sentences aloud and discussing the pictures. The more the children *hear* the words while looking at them, the greater will be their chance to develop automatic word recognition.

5. Try to assess the reasons for the children's errors and deal with them appropriately. Sometimes, as on the riddle pages, an error may be caused by faulty reasoning rather than by faulty decoding. At this stage, accurate decoding is a more important goal than perfect reasoning, and a child who decodes correctly but reasons poorly should still be praised for their reading.

6. Note that the "Yes" or "No" exercises and the "Draw a line" exercises are purposely written without clear-cut answers to every item. These pages should be discussed but not corrected. Make it a general rule *for all formats* not to put undue stress on getting the right answer. Instead, put the stress on accurate decoding and the enjoyment of using reading skills in a problem-solving situation.

Copyright © 2024, 2000, 1985, 1976, 1970, 1965, 1964 by the Estates of Donald E. Rasmussen and Lenina Goldberg. All rights reserved. Except as permitted under the United States Copyright Act, no part of this publication may be reproduced or distributed in any form or by any means, or stored in a database or retrieval system, without prior written permission from the publisher.

Email all inquiries to:
Peter Rasmussen, Editor
info@BasicReading.com

Website: BasicReading.com
ISBN 978-1-937547-05-9

__ed

bat	end	lift	nod	hunt
batted	ended	lifted	nodded	hunted

__ed

tag	spell	fill	rob	club
tagged	spelled	filled	robbed	clubbed

__ed

rap	peck	mix	chop	brush
rapped	pecked	mixed	chopped	brushed

__es

catch	dress	fix	box	buzz
catches	dresses	fixes	boxes	buzzes

1 — er

bat	lend	fix	box	buzz
batter	lender	fixer	boxer	buzzer
■	■	■	■	■
sad	fresh	sick	fond	gruff
sadder	fresher	sicker	fonder	gruffer
■	■	■	■	■
matter	better	bitter	copper	butter
scatter	letter	litter	proper	gutter
shatter	■	■	chopper	clutter
■	never	liver	■	shutter
banner	ever	river	bother	stutter
manner		shiver	■	■
■		■	robber	summer
gather		silver		■
rather				supper
■				■
ladder				rubber
■				
after				

__ est, __ ness

sad	fresh	sick	fond	gruff
■	■	■	■	■
sadder	fresher	sicker	fonder	gruffer
saddest	freshest	sickest	fondest	gruffest
■	■	■	■	■
sadness	freshness	sickness	fondness	gruffness

__ en

fat	red	stiff	rot	sunk
fatten	redden	stiffen	rotten	sunken
■	■	■	■	■
happen	seven	bitten	gotten	sudden
■		kitten	■	
Allen		mitten	oxen	
		■		
		linen		
		■		
		chicken		
		■		
		children		
		■		
		kitchen		

1

○ I mixed.
⊗ a mixer

○ the slippers
○ It slipped.

○ It's cracked.
○ a cracker

○ some ribbers
○ She rubbed.

○ a dropper
○ It dropped.

○ a bank
○ a banker

What is it?

 It is the hottest dinner.

 It is the fattest mitten.

What can she do?

 She can fix the robber's ladder.

 She can hunt and catch a robber.

What does she do?

 She helps the sickest ones.

 He prints the slickest ones.

What is he?

 He is the thinnest brother.

 He is the biggest drummer.

Who is he?

 He is a father and a singer.

○ He is a hunter and a shopper.

3 Helen is seven. She is bigger than her sister. She knows numbers and letters. She is printing some numbers and letters for her sister. Her sister is sitting by her.

"What happened?" said Helen to her sister.
"Something bit my mitten," her sister yelled back.
"I didn't know a mitten could be bitten," said Helen.

It was winter, and Helen was shivering. She wished that she had on rubbers and mittens.
"I must go back and get them," she said to herself.

Helen's sister is sad. She wished Helen would not go. But Helen said she would be back.
"When you get back, I'll stop being sad," her sister said.

1

Beth is getting sicker. She did not have any supper. Mother said, "If you rest, you will get —— ."

○ butter   ⊗ better   ○ batter

Ellen wanted to be a better catcher. Father said, Let's have some fun. You be the catcher and I'll be the —— ."

○ patcher   ○ pincher   ○ pitcher

Kim fixed two chickens. She said, "I can fix chickens. I am getting —— ."

○ better   ○ fixer   ○ batter

Dad was in the kitchen. He added butter to the mix and said, "I have to mix the batter until it gets —— ."

○ thicker   ○ quicker   ○ thicken

Jill's stuffed doll was ripped. Jill asked her mother, "Can my doll be —— ?"

○ fixer   ○ fixed   ○ fixes

1

Helen can be a sister,

   but can she be a mister?

   ○ Yes   ○ No

A dress can be matched,

   but can it be patched?

   ○ Yes   ○ No

A pet can be yanked,

   but can it be spanked?

   ○ Yes   ○ No

A pet can be a kitten,

   but can it be a mitten?

   ○ Yes   ○ No

A letter can be the thickest,

   but can it be the sickest?

   ○ Yes   ○ No

A glass can be cracked,

   but can it be tracked?

   ○ Yes   ○ No

A singer can sing in a rocker,

   but can she sing in a locker?

   ○ Yes   ○ No

I can swim in the river,

   but can I swim in the liver?

   ○ Yes   ○ No

Chickens and Children

	Yes	No
1. There are seven children bothering the hens.	○	⊗
2. The children are gathering the chickens' eggs.	○	○
3. One of the children is standing on the ladder.	○	○
4. The kitten has smashed the eggs to bits.	○	○
5. One chicken is running after another chicken.	○	○
6. The kitten is gathering up the eggs the fastest.	○	○
7. The chickens are cracking the eggs in the nests.	○	○

1 Ships can be docked in it.

Swimmers jump into it.

Fishermen catch dinner in it.

Is it — a runner / (a river) / a robber

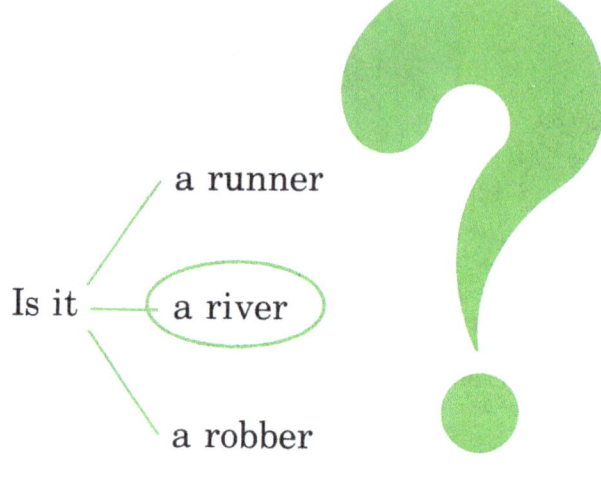

It is hatched from an egg.

It is bigger than a bug.

Children can have it for supper.

Is it — a camper / a shiver / a chicken

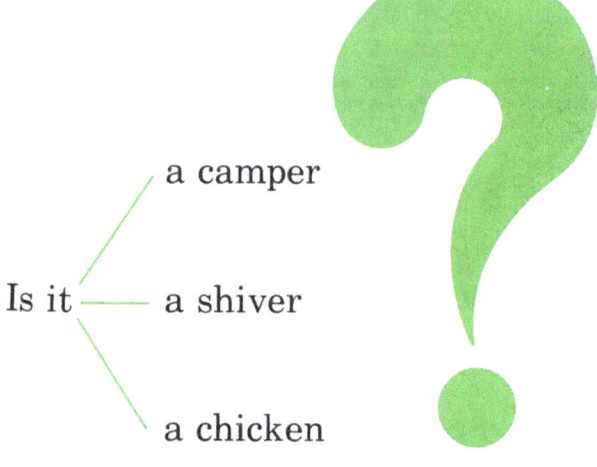

They are kept in the kitchen.

They cannot be mended if they are cracked.

Things can be spilled from them.

Are they — dishes / desks / drummers

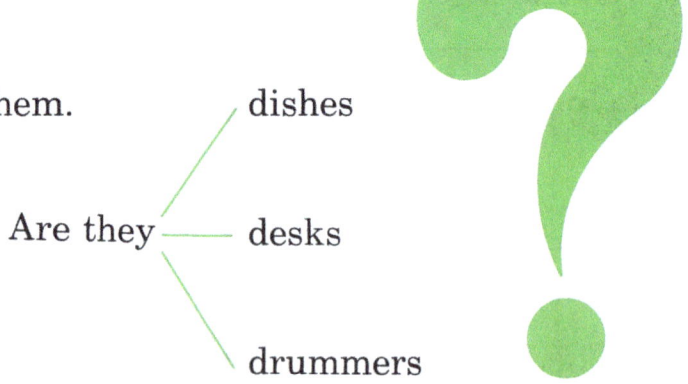

__y				
dad	pep	Bill	rock	pup
daddy	peppy	Billy	rocky	puppy

__ly				
sad	fresh	swift	hot	glum
sadly	freshly	swiftly	hotly	glumly

__ily				
happy			sloppy	lucky
■			■	■
happily			sloppily	luckily

__ies, __ied				
pansy	empty	lily	copy	study
pansies	empties	lilies	copies	studies
	■		■	■
	emptied		copied	studied

__le			__el	__al
candle	twinkle	apple	gravel	medal
handle	sprinkle	■	travel	pedal
■	■	saddle	■	■
fiddle	mumble	■	camel	metal
middle	tumble	little	■	petal
riddle	grumble	■	flannel	■
■		bottle	■	signal
pickle		■	level	
tickle		gobble	■	
		■	nickel	
		uncle	■	
			tunnel	

2

__ful				
thank	rest	fist	box	cup
thankful	restful	fistful	boxful	cupful

__on	__in	__ain
wagon	napkin	captain
dragon	■	
■	pumpkin	
cannon	■	
■	robin	
gallon		
■		
melon		

__et	__it	__ic	__ish
pocket	rabbit	picnic	finish
rocket	■	■	■
socket	visit	traffic	punish
■			■
comet			selfish
■			
puppet			
■			
ticket			

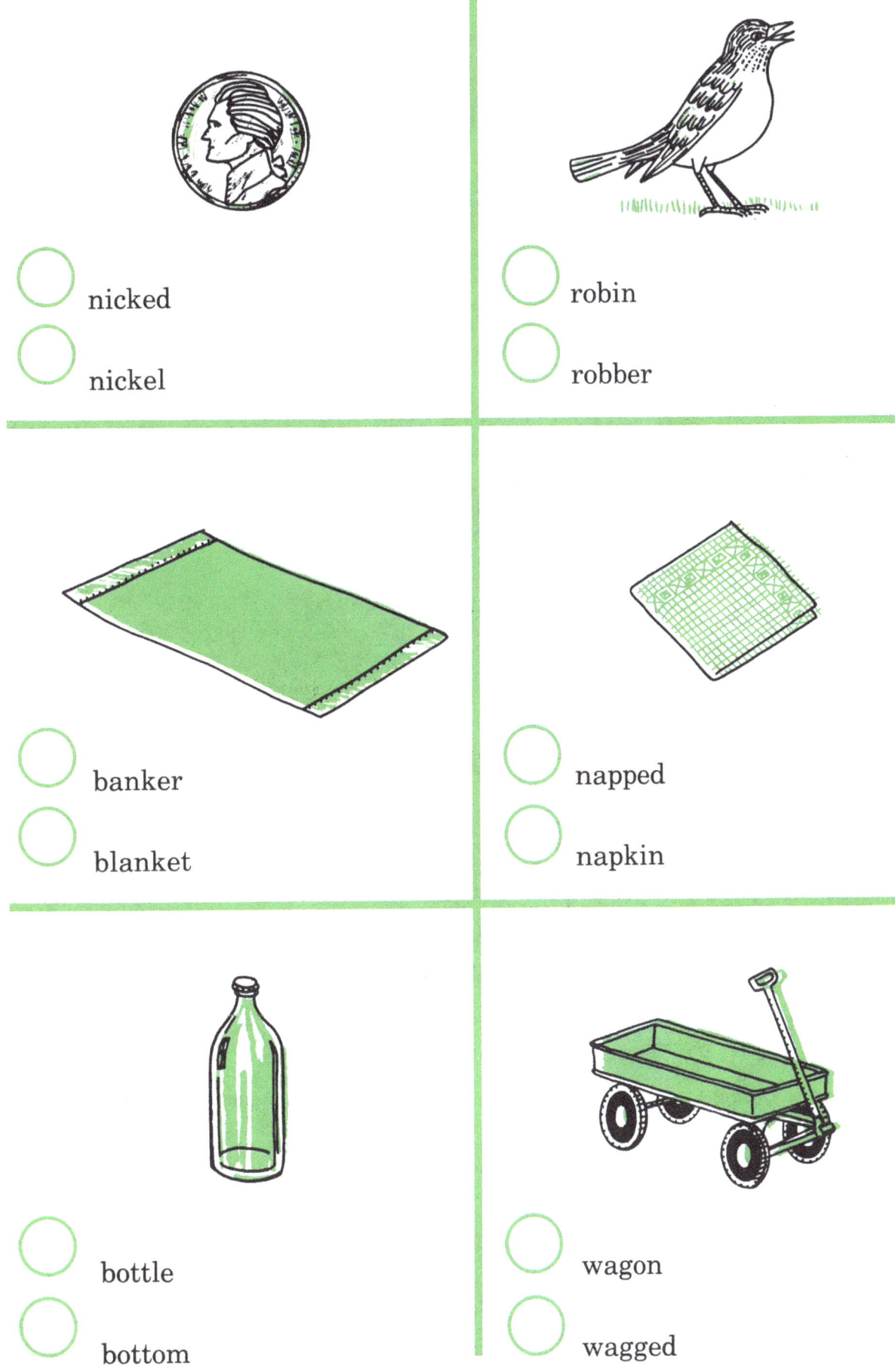

○ nicked
○ nickel

○ robin
○ robber

○ banker
○ blanket

○ napped
○ napkin

○ bottle
○ bottom

○ wagon
○ wagged

2

What can he do?

○ He can run and gobble.

○ He can jump and gallop.

What will she do?

○ She will sit in the saddle.

○ She will sit and study.

What is he doing?

○ He stumbles on the grassy hill.

○ He sprinkles the grass.

What did he do?

○ He went on a picnic with his mother.

○ He went on an errand for his mother.

What is she doing?

○ She is putting nuts into her jacket pocket.

○ She is putting shells into a sandy ditch.

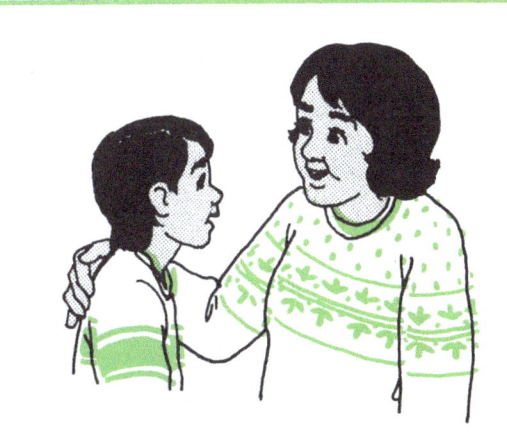

□ "We're getting a visitor," Mother said to Billy. "Your Uncle Andy is going to visit us."
Billy said, "Aren't we lucky? I'm happy he's coming to visit."

□ Uncle Andy had a pal with him. "This is Captain Locket," he said. The captain had a lot of medals.
"I'm happy to know you, Billy," said the captain.

□ Billy asked his uncle to help him finish his pumpkin.
"When it's finished, I'll put a candle in it," said Billy. "Won't that be jolly?"

□ Billy was sad when his uncle and the captain had to end the visit. He wanted to get presents for them. In the shop he asked, "What can I get for just a dollar?"

2

Billy wanted to get a puppy. He said, "I must empty my bank and get a lot of ——."

◯ pennies ◯ pansies ◯ puppets

Danny couldn't pick up the sprinkling can. He said, "I will have to fix the ——."

◯ helpful ◯ handy ◯ handle

Jimmy handed his mother a cupful of crackers. Mother said, "Thank you! You are very ——."

◯ helpful ◯ helper ◯ handful

The children were gathering rocks at the river. Betty said, "It is sunny. We are lucky it is not ——."

◯ foxy ◯ foggy ◯ fixed

The bus was stuck in the middle of the tunnel. Mr. Busman said, "I didn't want to be in this ——."

◯ traffic ◯ twinkle ◯ plastic

A kitty can get muddy,

but can it sit and study?

◯ Yes ◯ No

A puppy can be happy,

but can he be snappy?

◯ Yes ◯ No

A man can have a fiddle,

but can he do a riddle?

◯ Yes ◯ No

A man can travel quickly,

but can he travel sickly?

◯ Yes ◯ No

A lantern can have a candle,

but can it have a handle?

◯ Yes ◯ No

A box can get rusty,

but can it get dusty?

◯ Yes ◯ No

The grass can get sprinkled,

but can it get twinkled?

◯ Yes ◯ No

A chicken can tumble,

but can it mumble?

◯ Yes ◯ No

The Visitors

	Yes	No
1. There are twenty rabbits galloping on the grass.	○	○
2. One of the rabbits has tumbled into a bucket.	○	○
3. One of the rabbits is nibbling on a grassy patch.	○	○
4. The second rabbit is at the bottom of a tunnel.	○	○
5. An insect is trying to tickle the middle rabbit.	○	○
6. The children think the rabbits are funny.	○	○
7. A wagon is next to a bucket.	○	○

It has a hump.

It goes where it's sandy.

It travels where it's hot.

Is it
- a basket
- a camel
- a salad

It can be empty or filled.

It can get rusty.

Children want it for a present.

Is it
- a wagon
- a melon
- a whisper

It is little.

Someone can nibble on it.

It can have a red skin and a stem.

Is it
- a pebble
- an uncle
- an apple

__ee__

bee	feed	seen	deep	beet
see	need	green	keep	feet
wee	seed	queen	peep	meet
free	weed	screen	creep	sweet
tree	■	fifteen	sleep	street
three	feel	■	sweep	■
	heel	peek		seem
	wheel	seek		■
		week		needle
		cheek		

__ea__

pea	beat	team	meal	leaf
sea	heat	cream	real	■
tea	meat	dream	seal	leap
flea	neat	gleam	steal	■
■	seat	steam	■	weak
each	treat	scream	bean	■
beach	wheat	stream	lean	eager
peach	eat	■	mean	■
reach	■	beast	clean	eagle
teach	bead	feast		■
	lead	least		reason
	read	east		■
				beaver

20

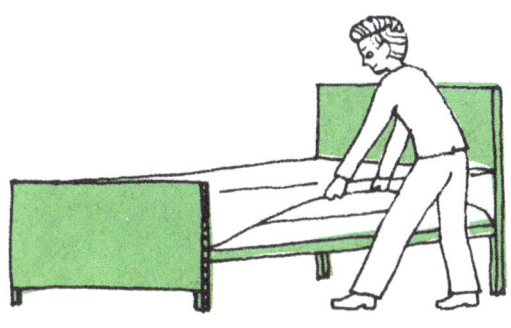

○ Dad helps by putting clean sheets on the bed.

○ Dad helps by cleaning the shelf by the bed.

○ The traveler is speeding.

○ The teacher is speaking.

○ Some puppies are on a team.

○ Some peaches are on a tree.

○ She is leaping it eagerly.

○ She is sleeping and dreaming.

○ Jean is feeding the eagle.

○ Jean is betting on the team.

○ The cattle are screaming.

○ The kettle is steaming.

3

3

Where will they go?

 to the bench to see the seal

 to the beach and the sea

What is she doing?

 She is clapping and ringing it.

 She is creeping to reach it.

What is he doing?

 He is lifting the seal.

 He is leaping into the sea.

What does he see?

 His brother is speeding up the street.

 A beaver is on the bank of a stream.

What does the teacher have?

 something to read to the children

 someone to reach the children

Father handed the twins some cash.
"Here is a nickel for each of you," he said. "You can get something sweet to eat. Then meet me on Peachtree Street."

"My wheel was stuck in a ditch," Father said. "Can you fix it?"
"It's easy to fix," said Jean. "But it won't be finished till next week."

The queen bee said to the other bees, "We have three jobs to do. Let's see whether we can do them speedily."
"What are the jobs?" the other bees asked.

"What do you want to see next?" the teacher asked.
"Let's see the seals," said the children. "We've seen the peacock and the camel, but we haven't seen the seals."

The children are eager to put the eggs in a basket. Jenny said, "We will have a candy egg —— ."

○ feet   ○ feast   ○ flea

3

Dad put the meat into the freezer. He said, "I'll get it when we need it for the next —— ."

○ meet   ○ mill   ○ meal

Jean had meat, beans, and peas to eat. She said, "After I eat my supper, I will have candy for a —— ."

○ treat   ○ tree   ○ team

Andy had his feet in the sand. He said, "It's fun on the —— ."

○ beach   ○ beat   ○ pitch

Billy scrubs his teeth after each meal. He said, "I feel better when I keep my teeth —— ."

○ steam   ○ clean   ○ green

A stream can be deep,

but can it creep?

○ Yes   ○ No

A doctor can treat,

but can he eat meat?

○ Yes   ○ No

A tree can be green,

but can it be seen?

○ Yes   ○ No

A bee can land on a peach,

but can it land on a beach?

○ Yes   ○ No

A seal can leap,

but can it sleep?

○ Yes   ○ No

A beast can be mean,

but can it be clean?

○ Yes   ○ No

A queen can drink tea,

but can she drink a bee?

○ Yes   ○ No

Your feet can creep,

but can they sweep?

○ Yes   ○ No

The Class Trip

	Yes	No
1. A man is feeding a meal to a seal.	○	○
2. The teacher and children can see the seal leaping.	○	○
3. The peacock is a mean beast and is hitting Jean.	○	○
4. Billy has reached the camel and is feeding it peanuts.	○	○
5. A beaver is next to the seal in the stream.	○	○
6. Jean can see the peacock from her seat.	○	○
7. Three sheep are reaching for the peanuts.	○	○

Jean can sleep on it.

Billy can dream on it.

Mother keeps it clean.

Is it — a street / a sheet / a sweep

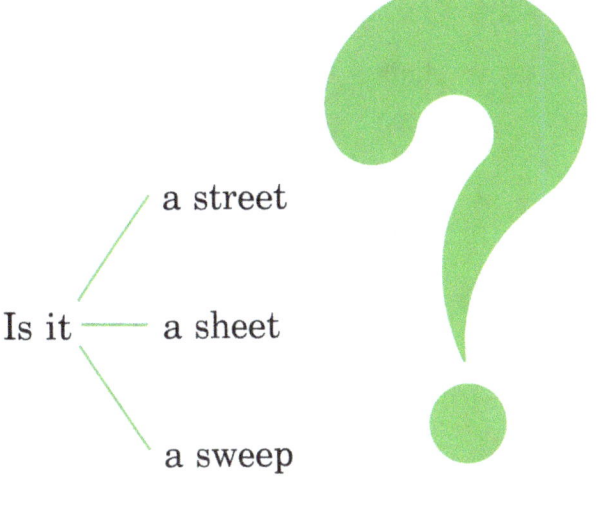

It is a big treat.

It is a big meal.

It is fit for a queen.

Is it — a feast / a flash / a freezer

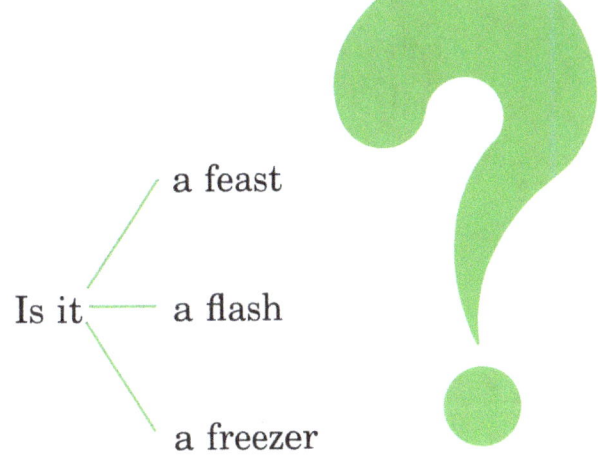

It is green.

You can see it on trees.

The wind can steal it.

Is it — a letter / a leap / a leaf

4

_ oo _

moo	boom	boot	hoop	food
too	room	hoot	loop	▪
zoo	bloom	root	scoop	roof
igloo	broom	toot	whoop	▪
▪	▪	shoot		tooth
moon	cool			▪
noon	tool			rooster
soon	spool			
spoon	stool			

_ ai _

fail	gain	brain	paid	daisy
hail	main	grain	▪	▪
mail	pain	train	maid	raisin
nail	rain	chain	▪	▪
pail		plain	maiden	aim
rail		stain	▪	
sail			wait	
tail			▪	
			waiter	
			▪	
			waist	

_ ay _

bay	clay	crayon
day	play	
gay	gray	
hay	pray	
may	tray	
pay	stay	
say	spray	
way	stray	

○ mail in a mailbag

○ milk in a milk pail

○ a doctor's crayon

○ a daisy chain

4

○ a painted spot

○ a tailor's spool

○ a pal of puppies

○ a pail of paint

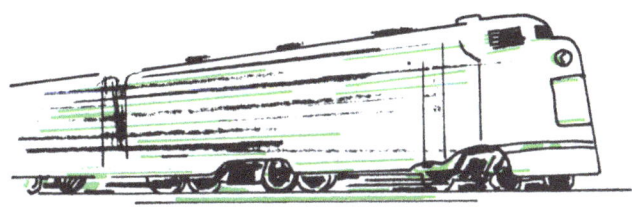

○ the roots of a plant

○ the boots of the rooster

○ a railway train

○ a playful team

What is he doing?

 He is mailing a letter.

 He is nailing the mailbox.

4

What does she have?

 She has a pail for her tools.

 She has a pain in her tooth.

What does it need?

 It needs a broom in a room.

 It needs a roof on the top.

Where are they?

 They are on a trip to the zoo.

 They are on the way to the moon.

What is she doing?

 She is yanking on her tooth.

 She is trying to get cooler.

Father was getting set to do some painting. He had a paint sprayer in his hand. Kay held the paint bucket.
"We'll spray the paint on," he said. "It's easier that way."

"I want to play in the rain," Jay said. "But I can't get my boots on my feet."
"Then you'll just have to play in your room," said Mother.

Mr. Spooner said, "I have a pain in my tooth."
"Then you should go to the dentist soon," said Mrs. Spooner. "You should go today. Don't wait."

"What does a rooster say?" Billy asked. "Does it say 'moo, moo'?"
"You know better than that," his father said. "A rooster says 'cock-a-doodle-doo.'"

May is waiting at the railway tracks. She is saying, "The best way to travel is by —— ."

○ tray ○ train ○ treat

The children are sitting on top of a haystack. They are saying, "We're going to stay here and —— ."

○ play ○ pail ○ pain

The two pals are painting the rocket ship. One is saying, "Soon we'll be zooming off to the —— ."

○ main ○ mean ○ moon

Gail is in her room painting. She is saying, "This is fun to do on a rainy —— ."

○ daisy ○ day ○ crayon

The waiter is waiting for them to say what they want to eat. The waiter is saying, "I'll bring the food on my —— ."

○ tray ○ trail ○ tooth

A letter can come in the mail,

but can it come in a pail?

○ Yes   ○ No

Children can see the moon,

but can they see it at noon?

○ Yes   ○ No

A sail is for a sailor,

but is it for a tailor?

○ Yes   ○ No

A man can wait in the rain,

but can he wait in a train?

○ Yes   ○ No

I can say "cock-a-doodle-doo,"

but can I say it in an igloo?

○ Yes   ○ No

A crayon can be gray,

but can it be clay?

○ Yes   ○ No

You can eat food on a stool;

can you eat it when it's cool?

○ Yes   ○ No

A painter can spray,

but can he play?

○ Yes   ○ No

The mailman's job is to bring the [1].

1. mail   2. hail

If you don't want to travel on a bus, you can travel on a [ ].

1. stain   2. train

If a chicken isn't a hen, it's a [ ].

1. roof   2. rooster

One thing everybody needs is [ ].

1. food   2. loops

If you drop food on your dress, you may get a [ ].

1. stain   2. sail

If you bump your leg, you may feel [ ].

1. pain   2. chain

Mother sweeps up the dust with a [ ].

1. gloom   2. broom

Children have lots of fun when they visit the [ ].

1. noon   2. zoo

Cows eat lots of grass and [ ].

1. gay   2. hay

When I asked if I could go, Mother said, "Yes, you [ ]."

1. may   2. pay

A Trip to the Beach

	Yes	No
1. The children are waiting for a train.	○	○
2. It is a gray and rainy day.	○	○
3. The children are playing on the beach.	○	○
4. Each of the children has a pail.	○	○
5. Mother and Father are going to sail to the moon.	○	○
6. Father dropped some nails and teaspoons from the basket.	○	○
7. Father may have some food in the picnic basket.	○	○

It has roots.

It can bloom.

You can pick one in May.

Is it
- a raisin
- a daisy
- a dress

4

It fits in a mailbag.

A mailman will bring it.

You may get one someday.

Is it
- a letter
- a player
- a trailer

Chickens can lay eggs in it.

You can play in it.

It is kept in stacks.

Is it
- clay
- ham
- hay

_oa_

boat	boast	coal	coach	soap
coat	coast	goal	roach	■
goat	roast	■	■	loaf
float	toast	load	loan	■
■		road	moan	roam
oats		toad		

_ou_

loud	found	pout	mouth	fountain
cloud	hound	shout	south	mountain
proud	pound	trout		
	round	out		
	sound			
	ground			

_ow_

cow	down	power	howl	crowd
bow	gown	tower	growl	■
how	town	flower	owl	powder
now	brown	shower		■
sow	clown			towel
	crown			

5

○ the gown
○ a goat

○ a toad
○ the toast

○ the seat
○ the soap

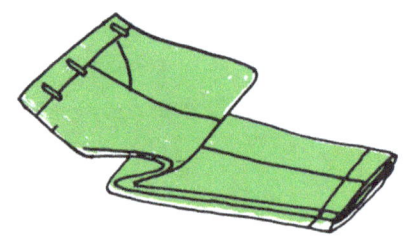

○ the towel
○ the trousers

○ a fountain
○ a flower

○ a cloud
○ a crowd

Where are the cows?

○ The cows can be found on the mountain.

○ The cows are south of the fountain.

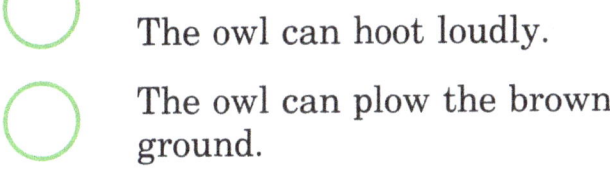

Where is it?

○ The soap is floating in the tub.

○ The float is stopping up the tub.

What can it do?

○ The owl can hoot loudly.

○ The owl can plow the brown ground.

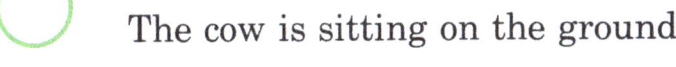

Where is it?

○ The cow is sitting on a crown.

○ The cow is sitting on the ground.

What did Dad do?

○ Dad clipped on his coat.

○ Dad slipped on the soap.

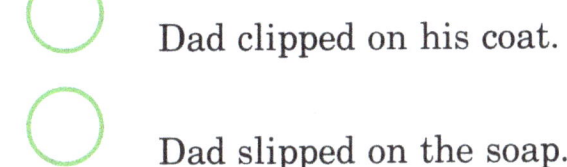

☐ The clouds in the sky were very black, and the ground was very dry. The flowers needed rain.
"I think we'll have a shower," said Mom.

☐ There wasn't a cloud in the sky. The sails of the boat were limp.
"We'd better aim for the coast now if we want to get there by noon," shouted the captain.

☐ Billy sat under the oak tree as the clouds drifted by. An oak leaf floated to the ground.
"That leaf means that winter is coming," said Billy.

☐ "Here's a towel, and here's some soap," Jim's father said to him. "Now get into the shower. I want you to be clean when we go downtown."

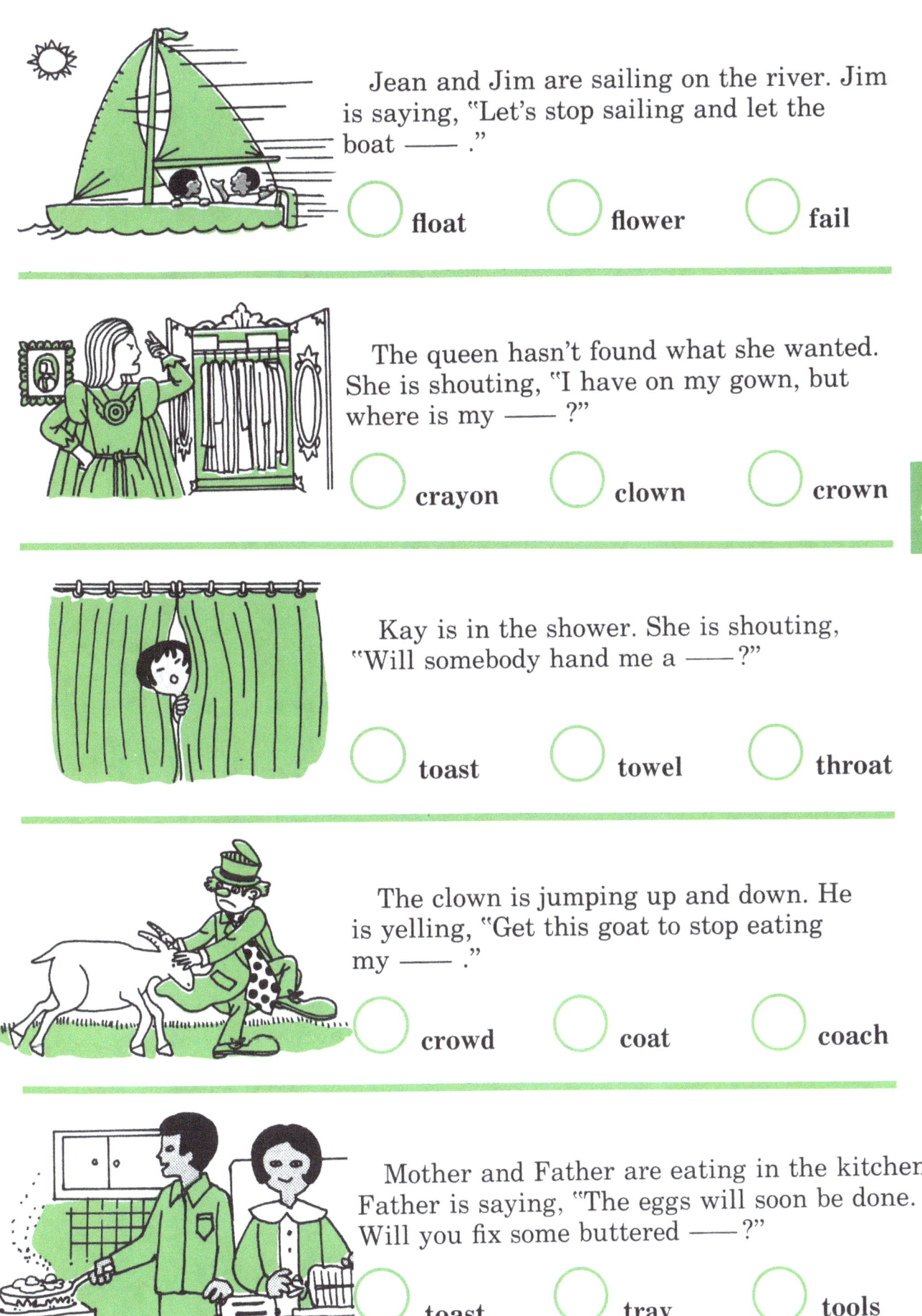

Jean and Jim are sailing on the river. Jim is saying, "Let's stop sailing and let the boat —— ."

○ float   ○ flower   ○ fail

The queen hasn't found what she wanted. She is shouting, "I have on my gown, but where is my —— ?"

○ crayon   ○ clown   ○ crown

Kay is in the shower. She is shouting, "Will somebody hand me a —— ?"

○ toast   ○ towel   ○ throat

The clown is jumping up and down. He is yelling, "Get this goat to stop eating my —— ."

○ crowd   ○ coat   ○ coach

Mother and Father are eating in the kitchen. Father is saying, "The eggs will soon be done. Will you fix some buttered —— ?"

○ toast   ○ tray   ○ tools

A sled can coast,

  but can it roast?

  ○ Yes   ○ No

A road can be in a town,

  but can it be in a crown?

  ○ Yes   ○ No

A clock can be round,

  but can it be wound?

  ○ Yes   ○ No

A clown can shout,

  but can he run out?

  ○ Yes   ○ No

A queen can have a crown,

  but can she have a gown?

  ○ Yes   ○ No

A goat can eat a coat,

  but can it eat a boat?

  ○ Yes   ○ No

Soap can be found in a shower;

  can it be found in a flower?

  ○ Yes   ○ No

A cow can be loud,

  but can it be proud?

  ○ Yes   ○ No

If you go camping, you may have to sleep on the ☐.

1. ground   2. found

Dad sent Mom a bunch of spring ☐.

1. flowers   2. crowds

You can't see the sun when it's hidden by the ☐.

1. clouds   2. proud

To get clean, you'll need a lot of ☐.

1. soap   2. toad

When you go out, put on your hat and ☐.

1. coat   2. shout

I can't swim, but I can ☐.

1. oats   2. float

Today I want to eat some eggs and buttered ☐.

1. coast   2. toast

A brown leaf fell from the tree to the ☐.

1. loud   2. ground

If you travel on the sea, you will travel on a ☐.

1. boat   2. coat

On her wedding day, my sister was dressed in a wedding ☐.

1. gown   2. growl

5

43

Billy and His Cow

	Yes	No
1. There are many flowers coming up from the ground.	○	○
2. A toad is growling at the cow.	○	○
3. A goat has a flower in its mouth.	○	○
4. Billy is shouting.	○	○
5. A clown is counting the flowers.	○	○
6. Billy has a rip in his trousers.	○	○
7. There is a big load of hay in back of the cow.	○	○

It can have brown spots on it.

It puts flowers in its mouth.

It can say "moo-moo."

Is it — a goat
— a cow
— a cat

You need it on a cloudy day.

You need it in a rain shower.

It fits on top of your jacket.

Is it — a railroad
— a fountain
— a raincoat

It can get the ground wet.

It is a shower.

It can be in the middle of town.

Is it — a mountain
— a fountain
— a raincoat

__aw__	
law	lawn
paw	yawn
saw	drawn
claw	crawl
draw	shawl
straw	awful
hawk	

__au__	
Paul	August
fault	

__oi__	
boil	joint
soil	point
toil	poison
broil	
spoil	
oil	

__oy
boy
joy
Roy
toy

__ie, __ies, __ied			
die	lie	pie	tie
dies	lies	pies	ties
died	lied		tied

__y, __ies, __ied				
cry	dry	fry	fly	try
cries	dries	fries	flies	tries
cried	dried	fried		tried

○ a hawk's claw

○ a hacksaw

○ Dad's yawn

○ Fred's drawing

○ the boiling milk

○ the coiling milk

○ the pointer

○ the poison

○ Paula feels the point.

○ It is Paula's fault.

○ The wind has died down.

○ The tent is tied down.

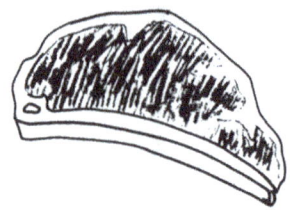

What will we do with it?

 We will broil it.

 We will coil it.

When is it best?

 It's best when it's soiled or spoiled.

 It's best when it's boiled or broiled.

What can it do?

 It can lie but cannot die.

 It can die but cannot tie.

What can it do?

 It can put poison on its claws.

 It can point its paw.

When do we have them?

 We have many of them in August.

 We have many of them in winter.

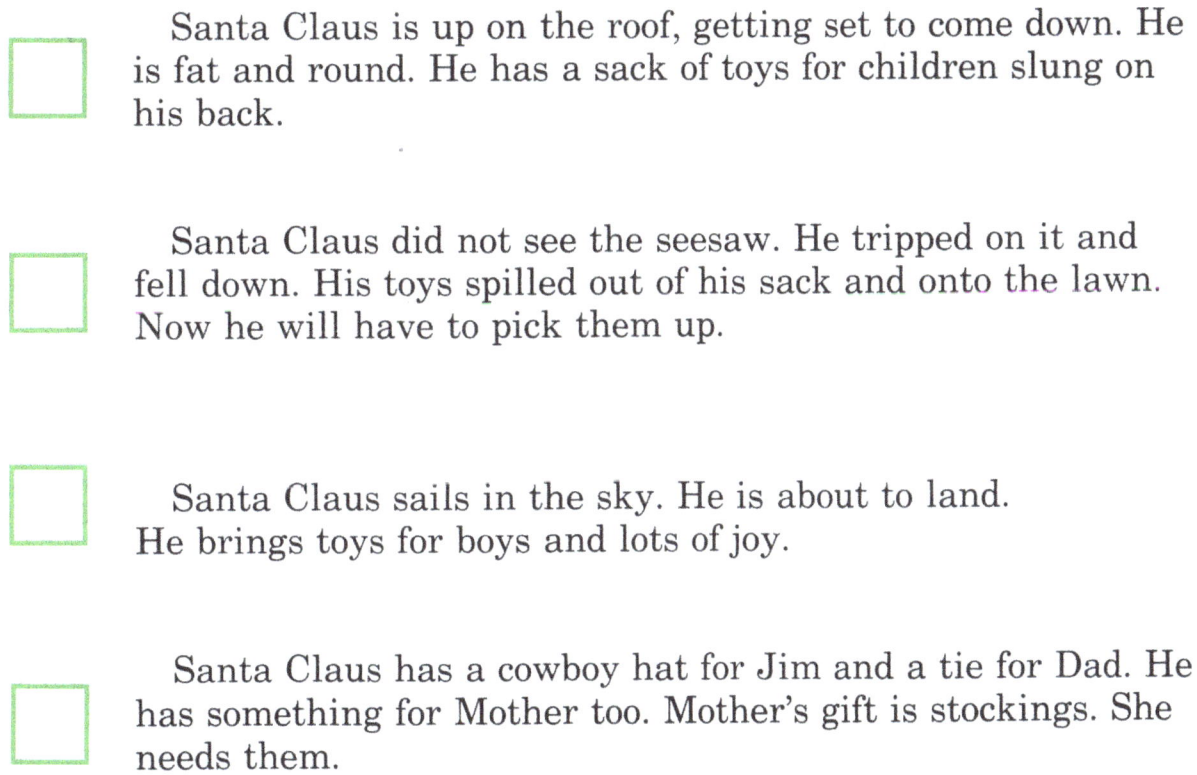

☐ Santa Claus is up on the roof, getting set to come down. He is fat and round. He has a sack of toys for children slung on his back.

☐ Santa Claus did not see the seesaw. He tripped on it and fell down. His toys spilled out of his sack and onto the lawn. Now he will have to pick them up.

☐ Santa Claus sails in the sky. He is about to land. He brings toys for boys and lots of joy.

☐ Santa Claus has a cowboy hat for Jim and a tie for Dad. He has something for Mother too. Mother's gift is stockings. She needs them.

Dad is putting straw on the lawn.
He thinks it will help the —— .

○ boil   ○ toil   ○ soil

Roy is boiling eggs in a pot. He would rather have them boiled than —— .

○ tied   ○ fried   ○ tried

Mom is tired. When she gets tired or sleepy, she —— .

○ yawns   ○ lawns   ○ dawns

Mom is putting soil into the flowerpot. She wishes to plant a —— .

○ fountain ○ flower   ○ shower

"You can't go into this shop," Paul is saying to his pup. "You must be —— ."

○ dried   ○ fried   ○ tied

A dress can be soiled,

but can it be broiled?

○ Yes   ○ No

A cow can be tied,

but can it be fried?

○ Yes   ○ No

A hawk has a claw,

but can it draw?

○ Yes   ○ No

A puppy can yawn,

but can it dig up a lawn?

○ Yes   ○ No

A rug can lie,

but can it die?

○ Yes   ○ No

A toy can be for a boy,

but does it bring him joy?

○ Yes   ○ No

Eggs can be boiled,

but can they be soiled?

○ Yes   ○ No

A tie can be tied,

but can it be dried?

○ Yes   ○ No

When the sun comes up, we say it is ☐.

1. claw   2. dawn

Mom said I could have some of that peach ☐.

1. pie   2. lie

This gun isn't real; it's just a ☐.

1. toy   2. joint

The spoon is bent, but it isn't my ☐.

1. August   2. fault

My pet rabbits sleep in a bed of ☐.

1. straw   2. draws

It rained, but my raincoat kept me ☐.

1. dry   2. fried

I don't think I can swim as fast as Jim, but I'll ☐.

1. try   2. ties

Mom sprayed the room to kill the ☐.

1. flies   2. dries

The men cut down the tree with an ax and a ☐.

1. yawn   2. saw

Dad said he would put some weed killer on the ☐.

1. lawn   2. crawl

52

A Picnic with the Grandchildren

	Yes	No
1. They are having a picnic on the lawn.	○	○
2. The man is broiling meat.	○	○
3. The grandchildren are sitting on a blanket.	○	○
4. They are going to have pie with the meal.	○	○
5. The puppy is tied to a tree to keep him from eating the food.	○	○
6. A hawk is sitting in the tree, waiting to steal some food.	○	○
7. The boy and his sister have many toys on the lawn.	○	○

It is flat and round.

We can eat it with a spoon.

We have it after dinner or supper.

Is it —— a pie
       —— a tie
       —— a lie

6 It flies in the sky.

It has claws on its feet.

Its bill is pointed.

Is it —— a hawk
      —— a lawn
      —— a cowboy

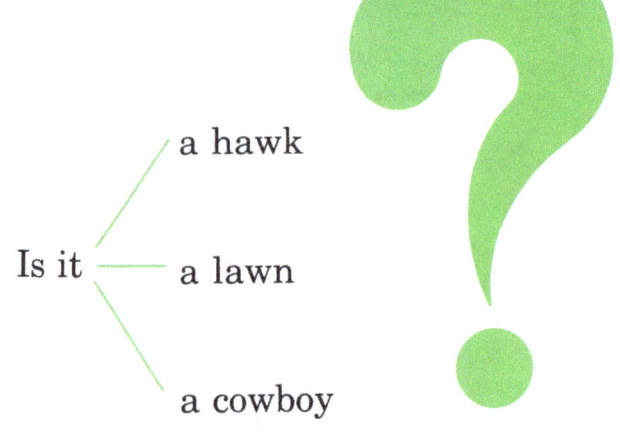

It has many teeth, but no mouth.

Oil will help to keep it slippery.

Dad keeps one in his tool shed.

Is it —— a saw
      —— a seesaw
      —— a paw

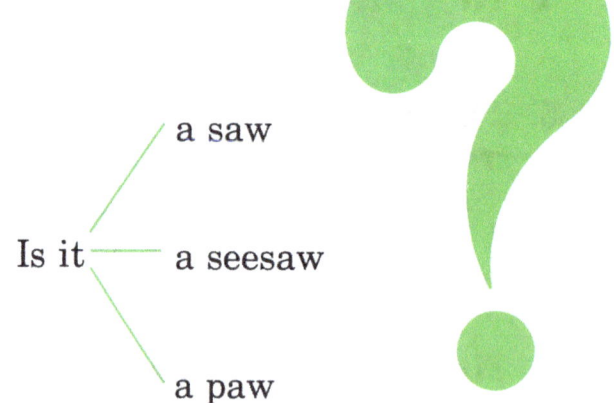

__ar	__al	__a	__ent
calendar	animal	Africa	different
caterpillar	hospital	camera	president
vinegar	several	Canada	resident

__y	__ble	__y
lullaby	possible	enemy
satisfy	terrible	family

a__	be__	de__	e__
about	begin	deliver	electric
afraid	begun	demand	eleven
agree	between	destroy	eleventh
allow	beyond		
America			
asleep			

pre__	re__
pretend	remember
present	repeat

7

- ○ She delivers letters to the family.
- ○ She delivers butter from Canada.

- ○ I'll remember the vinegar.
- ○ It's September on the calendar.

- ○ This is an electric clock.
- ○ This is the eleventh dock.

- ○ He's peeking at the animal.
- ○ He's asleep in the hospital.

- ○ The family is going to eat.
- ○ The enemy is going to repeat.

- ○ She retreated with a stick.
- ○ She remembered to get a ticket.

Where will he go?

○ He will rush to the camp of the enemy.

○ He will rush to an animal hospital.

Why is she crying?

○ She is afraid of the terrible dragon.

○ She is pretending to be a dragon.

What does the boy have?

○ He has seven different animals.

○ He has several toy animals.

Why is the boy running?

○ He is running for president.

○ He is delivering a letter.

What is he doing?

○ He is singing his sister to sleep.

○ He is pretending to be asleep.

7 ☐ Jean and Lee are packing some peaches, apples, and bananas in a basket. They are going on a picnic. As they pack the lunch, they are happily singing.

☐ Beyond the trees is a bench, and Lee has fallen asleep on it. Jean is picking flowers. As she picks, she counts them and thinks to herself, "I'll present them to Uncle Joe in the hospital. He has been sick. The flowers will make him happy."

☐ Several caterpillars are crawling about in the garden. "See how the caterpillars get around," said Jean. "Do you think they are trying to eat the flowers?"

☐ "The sky is cloudy and it's going to rain," said Jean. We'll get wet if we don't go back now." They begin running, but the rain begins to come down. Jean and Lee get terribly wet. But they are happy, for they have enjoyed the afternoon.

The belt on your trousers fits around your ☐.

1. waist   2. vinegar

When it rains, you must have an ☐.

1. umbrella   2. unhappy

When you're asleep, you have on your ☐.

1. presents   2. pajamas

If you were a hunter in Africa, you would hunt for ☐.

1. umbrellas   2. animals

If you were on a train, you would hand your ticket to a ☐.

1. comedian   2. conductor

If you enjoy going to the zoo, you will enjoy reading about the animals of ☐.

1. Africa   2. afraid

If you were gathering flowers, you could cut some ☐.

1. zinnias   2. vinegar

If you have a terrier, he may growl when the deliveryman brings a ☐.

1. lullaby   2. telegram

If you had a calendar, you could see that after August comes ☐.

1. September   2. America

If you want to get a snapshot, you will need a ☐.

1. caterpillar   2. camera

7

If you are seven,

   can you be eleven?

   ◯ Yes   ◯ No

If it rains today in Africa,

   can it rain today in Canada?

   ◯ Yes   ◯ No

A man can deliver a speech,

   but can he deliver a peach?

   ◯ Yes   ◯ No

My mom can sing a lullaby,

   but can she sing a satisfy?

   ◯ Yes   ◯ No

A cow can run between two cats;

   can it run beyond two rats?

   ◯ Yes   ◯ No

A salad may need vinegar,

   but does it need a calendar?

   ◯ Yes   ◯ No

A camera will snap shots,

   but can it snap pots?

   ◯ Yes   ◯ No

A president can be defeated,

   but can he be repeated?

   ◯ Yes   ◯ No

What's it about?

Linda and Beth were pretending to be travelers who had just met on a ship.

"I left my family back in Africa," said Beth. "I'm on my way to Canada."

"How interesting," said Linda. "Canada will seem very different from Africa, but you'll enjoy it. What will you do there?"

"I'm a doctor. I'll be running a big hospital. What about you?"

"I keep caterpillars," said Linda. "I sell the silk that the caterpillars spin. It's interesting. Will you visit me in America?"

"I will!" Beth agreed.

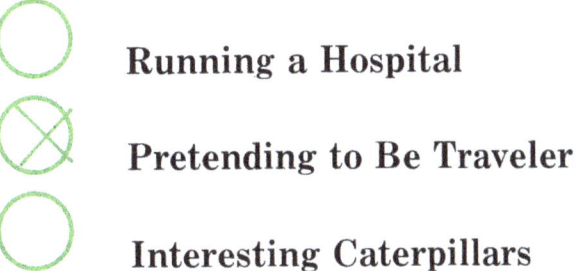

○ Running a Hospital

⊗ Pretending to Be Travelers

○ Interesting Caterpillars

Jean enjoys drawing flowers. She copies the daisies and zinnias Mother planted next to the lawn.

"I will select my green crayon for the lawn," said Jean, "and my red crayon for the zinnias."

"Remember to put in a tree, too," said Mother, "and the trunk should be brown."

"Maybe I will put a stream between the flowers and the tree," said Jean. "And beyond the stream, I will draw some mountains. Then my drawing will be interesting."

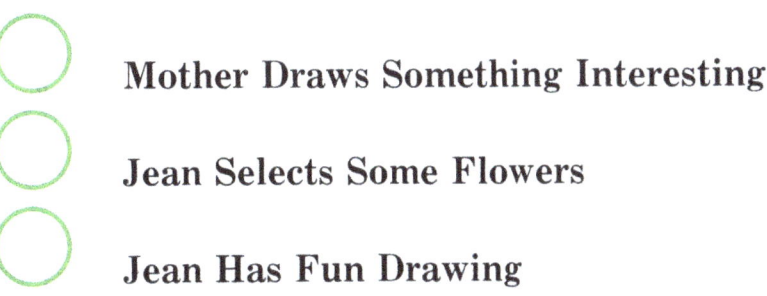

○ Mother Draws Something Interesting

○ Jean Selects Some Flowers

○ Jean Has Fun Drawing

Some letters were ☐, so the mailman could not ☐ them.

1. deliver   2. destroyed

Tim was ☐ the ☐ train he got from Santa Claus.

1. enjoying   2. electric

The boy was reading something ☐ about ☐.

1. interesting   2. Indians

Jim was ☐ with ☐ of the presents he got from Santa Claus.

1. several   2. satisfied

Jim didn't know which ☐ to select for the ☐ of his class.

1. present   2. president

The ☐ was ☐ the stool and could not be seen.

1. underneath   2. umbrella

Mother went shopping to ☐ ☐ presents for Dad.

1. select   2. several

Father ☐ his trip on the fast ☐ train.

1. express   2. enjoyed

Joan's pet ☐ had a ☐ loud growl.

1. terribly   2. terrier

The boys ran ☐ the trees and ☐ the big hill.

1. between   2. beyond

7

62

The Children Help a Train Conductor

One September afternoon, Kay and Jack were playing on a hill by some railroad tracks. There was a loud crash. They ran to see where the sound had come from. The wheels of a train had jumped the tracks. Kay and Jack saw that the conductor needed help and should get to a hospital. Kay sped back to her family to get some help. Her big sister went with her to the railroad tracks.

"I'm afraid we'll have to get you to the hospital," Kay's sister said to the conductor.

"Will you let us go with you?" asked Kay and Jack. Kay's sister agreed and they were on the way.

When the conductor was better, he remembered how much Kay and Jack had helped him. He wanted to get them a present. He selected an electric train set for the children. "I can't think of a better way to express my thanks," he said to them. Kay and Jack enjoyed the electric train set. There were several different trains. They put them on the tracks and let them go round and round. "We really enjoy this present," they said.

	Yes	No
1. The children helped the train conductor.	○	○
2. The conductor had to go to the hospital.	○	○
3. The children got a present from the train conductor.	○	○
4. The conductor didn't thank the children.	○	○
5. There were several different trains in the train set the children got as a present.	○	○
6. Kay's sister went to the tracks to see the conductor.	○	○

You need it on rainy days.

You stand underneath it when it rains.

You keep it shut until you go out.

Is it
- an uncle
- an umbrella
- an animal

It crawls on the ground.

It enjoys having a leaf for dinner.

It becomes a butterfly.

Is it
- a calendar
- a camera
- a caterpillar

You put them on in the bedroom.

You have them on when you're asleep.

If you're sick in the hospital, you will need them.

Are they
- pajamas
- presents
- presidents

_a_e

date	bake	came	made	cape
gate	cake	game	blade	grape
hate	lake	name	grade	shape
late	make	same	shade	scrape
skate	flake	blame	trade	escape
plate	shake	flame	parade	ape
ate	awake	became	lemonade	■
■	mistake			chase
cave				■
gave				taste
save				
wave				
forgave				

_i_e

fine	dime	hide	bite	file
line	time	ride	kite	mile
mine	■	slide	quite	pile
nine	five	beside	white	smile
vine	hive	divide	invite	awhile
shine	drive	inside	polite	
valentine	alive			
	arrive			

_o_e

joke	bone	hose	hole	drove
woke	cone	nose	pole	stove
broke	shone	rose	stole	
smoke	stone	chose	▪	
spoke	throne	close	note	
awoke	alone	those	vote	
		suppose		

_u_e

rude	use
crude	excuse
include	▪
▪	cube
June	tube
tune	
▪	
rule	

_e_e

Pete	Steve
complete	eve
concrete	▪
	these

8

○ Pete takes a bite.

○ Pete beats the cake mix.

○ Dave trades his clock.

○ Dave tells his teacher the time.

○ He's inside his home.

○ He's beside the hole.

○ He's playing hide-and-seek.

○ He's baking a cake.

○ The ruler is on his throne.

○ He knows the rules of the game.

○ He has a valentine.

○ He has nine vines.

The cowboys are

○ using the thin file to make paint.

○ using the campfire to make pancakes.

The campers are

○ homesick and want to go home.

○ at home packing a case.

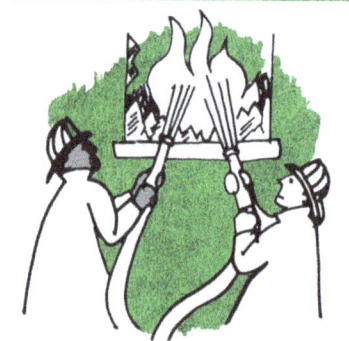

The firemen have to

○ have cones as they sit beside the fire.

○ get close to the blaze to put out the flames.

The sisters are

○ riding beside each other.

○ hiding dimes from mother.

The clown is speaking to

○ the king, who is sitting on a shiny throne.

○ the king, who is shining his throne.

Faye swung her bat for the second time.
"Strike two," yelled the catcher.
"I don't want to strike out this time," said Faye.
She swung at the next pitch and began to run.
"It's a hit! It's a hit!" yelled Faye's teammates.

Steve was shopping in a bakery. He pointed to a little cake on the shelf. "May I have that pineapple cake?" he asked the baker.
"Yes, if you have five dimes in your pocket," said the baker.
Steve put his hand in his pocket and said, "I don't have any dimes in my pocket. I just have a hole."

Mike came running inside to see his mother. "Mother, do you have any string? I need some to fly my kite."
Mother found some string and gave it to Mike.
"Thanks," said Mike. "I'll make a tail for the kite and tie this string to the frame. Then I can fly it."

"Let's play hide-and-seek," Kate said to her playmate.
"Fine!" said Joan. "You wait while I hide. Then you try to find me."
Joan ran to hide, and Kate began to count. When she had counted up to a hundred by fives, she yelled, "Here I come!"

The flag was flying on top of the pole. Dave said to his teacher, "I can see the flag. It has many white —— ."

○ straps ○ stripes ○ strips

The beach was many miles away from home. But Jane and Dave were not homesick. "I like it here," said Jane, smiling. "There are piles of sand and the sun is —— ."

○ shining ○ shading ○ sizing

"The train is arriving on track number nine," said the conductor on the loudspeaker.
"Let's go quickly," said Jane. "We mustn't be —— ."

○ lifted ○ led ○ late

"I can't get up the driveway," said Father. "There's something in the way. It must be a pile of —— ."

○ stones ○ stoves ○ stoles

"I suppose I need an envelope," said Pam. "Yes you do, if you want to mail that —— ."

○ nose ○ neat ○ note

An ape can hide in a cave,

but can it ride on a wave?

○ Yes   ○ No

A boy can chase a snail,

but can he chase a whale?

○ Yes   ○ No

If a boy knows how to shave,

does he know how to be brave?

○ Yes   ○ No

A plane can fly for many miles,

but can it fly in sandpiles?

○ Yes   ○ No

We don't have the same name,

but can we play the same game?

○ Yes   ○ No

If a man tells a joke,

can you say that he spoke?

○ Yes   ○ No

I can get nine roses,

But can I get nine noses?

○ Yes   ○ No

A man can close a gate,

but can he close a plate?

○ Yes   ○ No

A Fine Time

Kate had just met Jane.

"Mother," she said, "May I invite Jane to come home with me? She seems like a fine playmate!"

"What games will you play?" Mother asked.

"We'll set up a lemonade stand. We'll sell lemonade and grape drink. We'll make some dimes that way."

"That's fine," said Mother. "My sister Eve and I used to do that when we were little. That's how we became interested in trade. We saved what we made. Today we run a chain of shops, as you know."

"I know, Mother," Kate said. "And that's what I want to do when I am big."

"Does Jane want to be a shopkeeper too?"

"No," said Kate. "She'd rather drive a bus. But she wants to help sell lemonade just the same."

"Well, bring Jane home with you. I hope you have a fine time."

	Yes	No
1. Kate met her mother at the gate.	○	○
2. Kate was planning to sell lemonade.	○	○
3. Kate's mother had a sister named Jane.	○	○
4. Kate's mother and her sister ran a chain of shops.	○	○
5. Jane would rather drive a bus than run a shop.	○	○
6. Mother did not want Kate to invite Jane to her home.	○	○

When you do something you're afraid to do, you are ☐.

1. brave   2. blamed

If you are polite, you will invite your pal to visit your ☐.

1. ham   2. home

If you have ten pennies, you can trade them for a ☐.

1. dime   2. date

The best time to play outside is in the ☐.

1. daytime   2. bedtime

If you are going on a picnic, you can take a jug of ☐.

1. lullabies   2. lemonade

Twins can be two brothers who are the same ☐.

1. smile   2. size

When you are away from home for a while, you can become ☐.

1. homesick   2. hidden

The king who sits on the throne and rules the land is a ☐.

1. ruler   2. rider

A cake and a drum sometimes have the same ☐.

1. shape   2. scale

When the sun shines on you, you get under a tree to be in the ☐.

1. shade   2. shape

73

Draw a line under the things that can make you smile.

a joke	a slide
a game	a bite
a flame	a prize

Draw a line under the things that are fun to have at playtime.

paste	a slide
skates	a wagon
a shade	a gate

Draw a line under the things that you can hide.

a dime	a rope
a mine	a throne
a bone	a home

Draw a line under the things that can be closed.

a home	a plane
a rope	a gate
a case	a stone

Draw a line under the things that can wake you up.

a scale	the sunshine
a clock	a kite
a shake	a hole

Draw a line under the things that can be broken.

a wife	a mile
a vase	a kite
a stove	a rake

Draw a line under the things that can tell you there's a fire.

smoke	a fire truck
a cape	flames
a case	a blaze

Draw a line under the things that you can do outside.

drive	wake up
bake	skate
hide	ride

What's it about?

Sal and Ben were fishing in a lake.

"It must be time to have lunch," said Sal. "Let's eat."

"Fine," said Ben.

"But I smell smoke. We'd better go see where it's coming from," said Sal.

"Someone may have made a mistake and left a fire untended," said Ben.

"Yes," said Sal. "We'd better run and see."

So they ran until they saw some smoke. "There's the fire, next to the cave," yelled Sal, pointing to the left.

"What flames!" yelled Ben. "We must put them out. What shall we do?"

"We can fill some pails at the lake," said Sal. "That way we can put out the fire quickly." And they did!

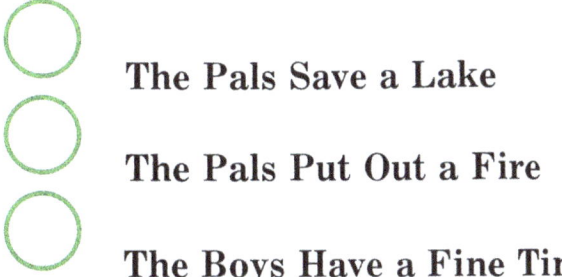

○ The Pals Save a Lake

○ The Pals Put Out a Fire

○ The Boys Have a Fine Time

Sal and Ben each held a fishing pole as they sat on a dock beside the lake. The fishing lines were in the lake. Each pal wanted to catch a fish. "I like this fishing pole that Mother gave me," said Ben.

"I like mine too," said Sal. "But I wish we'd catch a fish."

"Maybe if I get closer, I'll catch a fish," said Ben.

As time passed and not a thing happened, Ben said, "We won't catch any fish today."

"Yes we will," whispered Sal. "I feel a tug on my line," And five seconds later, Sal had a fish hanging from the end of her line.

"There's something tugging on mine too," said Ben. Ben tugged eagerly on his line. Then he yelled, "I've got a fish!"

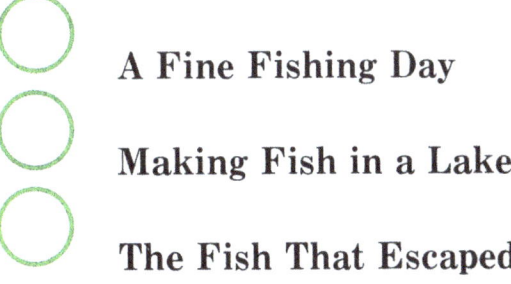

○ A Fine Fishing Day

○ Making Fish in a Lake

○ The Fish That Escaped

Mr. Slade began to ☐ his plate so Wag could have some ☐.

1. scraps   2. scrape

Mother said, "Your ☐ today is to ☐ the cake that I baked."

1. taste   2. task

The children went up the ☐ and then ☐ down it.

1. slide   2. slid

Do you think a ☐ can splash ☐ it swims?

1. while   2. whale

Mother and Father have a ☐ to take a ☐ trip.

1. plan   2. plane

Rose asked, "Mother, may James and I ☐ the paste you just gave ☐?"

1. us   2. use

"Dave is not ☐ willing to ☐ the game yet," said the pitcher.

1. quite   2. quit

Kate had a big ☐ of sand beside her, but it didn't fit into her ☐.

1. pail   2. pile

"When you come to my home, I will ☐ you to play ☐ with me," Jane said to her playmate.

1. invite   2. inside

"We must wait for Father to ☐ the ☐ out of your skate, Betty," said Mother.

1. take   2. tack

8

The Tale of an Ape That Escaped

James was a fine animal keeper. He had a job in the big zoo. He kept Ricky the ape safe and happy.

James did his job well. But one day he had a terrible time with Ricky. As James was driving the zoo truck down the street, taking Ricky to a parade, something began to bang in the back of the truck.

James stopped the truck to see what it was. Ricky was not in the back. James saw the ape running down the road.

"Ricky the ape has escaped," yelled James. "Stop, Ricky! Stop!"

But Ricky just kept on running. James began to chase him, but he was afraid he couldn't catch him. Apes can run fast for many miles.

"I must catch him!" puffed James. And he bravely kept on chasing Ricky. "If I can get close to him, I can catch him with my rope."

Suddenly, Ricky was nowhere to be seen. James ran up to the spot where he had last seen Ricky and stopped. There he saw Ricky in a deep ditch. Ricky couldn't get out.

With his rope, James tugged Ricky to safety and put him back in the zoo truck. Then James began driving Ricky to the parade.

"I think Ricky would rather be in a big parade than down in a ditch," James said to himself with a smile.

	Yes	No
1. Ricky was an ape that escaped from a zoo truck.	○	○
2. James was a zookeeper who put snakes and whales in ditches.	○	○
3. James was taking the ape to trade him for a beaver.	○	○
4. James chased the ape down the road and tried to catch him.	○	○
5. The ape fell into a lake and got out by himself.	○	○
6. James got the ape back into the zoo truck and drove off to the parade.	○	○

It has hoses and ladders on it.

Brave men stand on the back of it.

The driver can make it go quite fast.

Is it — a flower / a fountain / a fire truck

You can draw it with a pen.

You can use a ruler to make it.

You can make it many sizes.

Is it — a loan / a line / a life

It is a home for bees.

Bees make food in it.

The food they make in it is sweet and sticky.

Is it — a hive / a hose / a hoop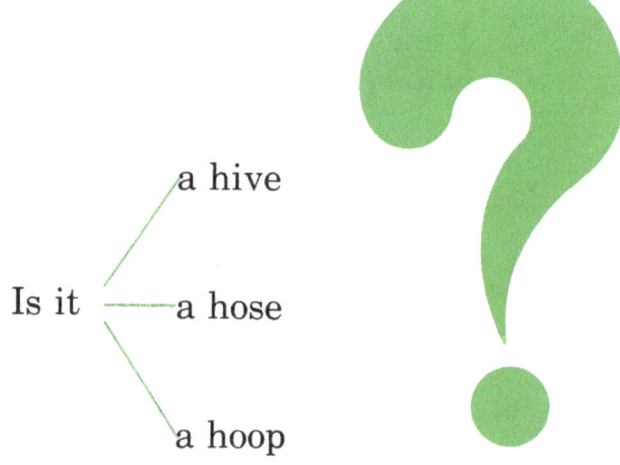

_a_	
lazy	able
crazy	table
baby	stable
lady	cradle
bacon	aviator
	alligator
apron	radiator

_e_	
Steven	zebra
even	secret
evening	tepee
evil	Peter
Sweden	

_i_	
find	lion
kind	dandelion
mind	tidy
blind	tiger
grind	spider
behind	
mild	pilot
wild	
child	

_u_	
music	truth
pupil	ruin
tulip	July

o		ou
cold	hero	soup
fold	zero	group
gold	■	■
sold	potato	wound
told	tomato	
scold	■	

		ow
old	radio	
■	■	mow	fellow
roll	auto	row	yellow
toll	■	bow	■
troll	hello	low	shadow
■	■	blow	■
most	ago	crow	window
post		grow	
■		show	
poster		slow	
■		snow	
pony		throw	
■			
open			
■			
only			

9

○ He sits on the windowsill.

○ He sits below the elevator.

○ Joy is towing a boat.

○ Joy is rowing a boat.

○ Susan is painting a poster.

○ Susan is protecting her pony.

○ The potato is rolling in the bowl.

○ The puppy is rolling in the snow.

○ Mother throws a shadow.

○ Mother opens the window.

○ A child sees the lion in the zoo.

○ A child is kind to the zebra.

 **Mr. Olds is opening**

 the gas tank behind the shop.

 the gate behind the ponies' stable.

 **The child sees**

 the wild lion rolling over.

 the wild lady reaching over.

 **Ruth is**

 showing her mother the violets.

 skating slowly behind her mother.

 **There is only**

 one dandelion growing in the grass.

 one alligator rowing in the lake.

 **Mr. Stevens put on an apron**

 and began to pick ripe tomatoes.

 and began to boil the potatoes.

☐ One day Judy helped her Dad with the shopping. They got tomatoes, bacon, eggs, and soup. At the checkout counter, the owner of the shop sold them the food and told them, "That soup is just the thing for a cold day like today."

☐ When Judy and her dad had finished shopping, they went home. At home, Dad opened the bag of tomatoes. "They're not ripe yet," he said. "Let's put them on the windowsill to ripen. When the tomatoes are red, they will be fine in a salad.

☐ Judy was playing in her room one cold day. She pretended to be the hero of a TV show she had seen. She told her dog, "I know your evil secret, Fido. You are really the Spider Lady cleverly dressed as a dog."

☐ Judy had a cold and had to stay in her room. She sat by the window and watched the children playing in the snow. They were having such fun! Judy said, "If only I didn't have this cold, I could play in the snow too. Staying in is driving me crazy!"

Amy went to see a show.
"There's only one seat," she said. "It's in the ninth ——."

○ road   ○ row   ○ roll

"Where is your pony, Rudy?" asked his father.
Rudy said, "He is next to your colt in the ——."

○ stake   ○ shadow   ○ stable

The tiny child was in the cradle.
Her big brother told a pal, "She just came home from the hospital. She is a tiny ——."

○ bakery   ○ baby   ○ bacon

"What kind of animals do you have in this zoo?" asked Ruth.
   The zookeeper said, "We have tigers, apes, snakes, and ——."

○ lions   ○ lemons   ○ ruins

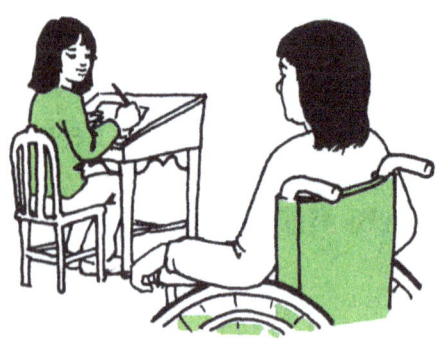

Mother asked, "Sue, are you able to help me now? I need a pint of milk and a pound of ——."

○ bank   ○ bacon   ○ bands

A colt can grow up in a stable,

but can it grow up on a table?

○ Yes ○ No

A funny poem can be told,

but can a funny poem be old?

○ Yes ○ No

A tulip can be gold or yellow,

but can a tulip be a fellow?

○ Yes ○ No

The wind can blow and blow,

but can it grow and row?

○ Yes ○ No

Mother can fry potatoes,

but can she fry tomatoes?

○ Yes ○ No

The wind blows snowflakes down,

but can it blow them into town?

○ Yes ○ No

Potatoes can be tasted,

but can potatoes be pasted?

○ Yes ○ No

Lions and tigers can bite,

but can they be white?

○ Yes ○ No

The Flying Postman

Ken was a flying postman. He delivered the mail even on snowy days. Ken was a fine aviator and was able to fly even when it was very cold. There were times when it snowed and the wind and snow were blinding.

Ken had an errand to run. He was to fly to Middletown. He had valuable mail to deliver. He began his trip on a fine winter evening. On the way, however, it began to snow and when he gazed out the window, he saw that the snow had slowed his plane.

"Maybe I'm close to a landing strip," said Ken. "I'll use my radio, and perhaps I can get help." For a while it was silent, but after the ninth try a sound came over the radio.

"Hello, Ken, you may land at the Mapleton strip. Bring the plane down slowly." Ken did this and finally landed.

Both Ken and the fellow who had helped him agreed that it was not easy to pilot a plane in the snow.

Later, when it was not cloudy, Ken was able to take his plane up and was on his way. He finally reached Middletown with the mail. His trip was completed.

	Yes	No
1. Ken the aviator wouldn't fly his plane when it was cold outside.	○	○
2. Ken had to fly his mail plane to Middletown.	○	○
3. The snow slowed down the plane.	○	○
4. The radio in Ken's plane was broken.	○	○
5. Ken said it was easy to land a plane in the blinding snow.	○	○
6. Ken was able to land the plane slowly on the strip.	○	○

I fly a plane.

Some say I'm an aviator.

I can fly a jet or a plane with propellers.

Am I — a postman
      — a pilot
      — a pillow

It is in your dining room.

You can put bowls and plates of food on it.

After dinner it can be very untidy.

Is it — a lion
     — a table
     — a cradle

I have not grown up yet.

I sleep in a cradle.

My playpen folds up.

Am I — a baby
     — a berry
     — a lady

If you are a boy, you can grow up to be a ☐.

1. propeller   2. postman

If you don't help your mother keep your home tidy, she may say you are ☐.

1. lazy   2. lady

If you like music, you may want to play a ☐.

1. violin   2. violet

A blanket keeps you from getting cold and is something you can ☐.

1. flow   2. fold

A bug that spins a web is a ☐.

1. spider   2. spade

Father tells his children different tales every ☐.

1. evening   2. elevator

If the sun isn't shining, you may not be able to see your ☐.

1. shadow   2. show

Sometimes, after it rains, you may see a ☐.

1. remember   2. rainbow

A pony eats hay in a ☐.

1. cradle   2. stable

If you had sprained your hip, it would be ☐.

1. swollen   2. sold

Draw a line under the names you may see on a calendar.

Friday	November
July	postman
hotel	April

Draw a line under the things that grow.

babies	shows
colts	violets
tables	tomatoes

Draw a line under the things you may find on a table.

a bowl	a hotel
potatoes	tomatoes
a window	gold

Draw a line under the things that may be sold.

clocks	tigers
moments	Friday
rolls	pillows

Draw a line under the things that are flowers.

tulips	dandelions
spiders	violets
goldenrod	ponies

Draw a line under anything that may be yellow.

a shadow	an apron
a dandelion	a window
a tomato	a pillow

Draw a line under the things that tell us it's cold outside.

a snowman	a pillow
china	frozen windows
snowflakes	a maple tree

Draw a line under the things that are grown-up.

a pilot	an old fellow
a baby	a colt
a lady	a child

What's it about?

My teacher told us we were going to the zoo on Friday, October the ninth. We had studied tales about the wild animals. But now we were going to see real zebras and alligators. We would see tigers and lions, and camels and apes! My class was very happy to be going to the zoo.

Finally the day came, and we eagerly began the trip. It was fun seeing the lions and tigers. The zebra was so playful, running and galloping for us. We liked the apes, too, but we were told not to throw anything to them. The day was really fun for us.

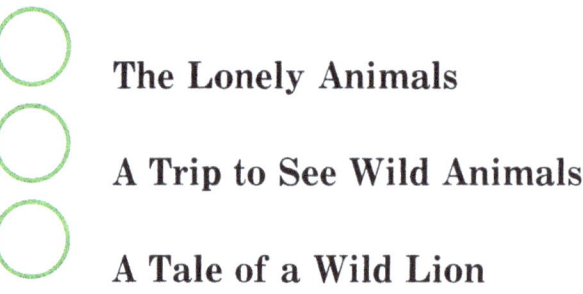

○ The Lonely Animals

○ A Trip to See Wild Animals

○ A Tale of a Wild Lion

One day Jay asked his father to take him to see a plane. They arrived at the runway and met one of the pilots. Jay and the pilot went up to the plane. He showed Jay the propellers. They went inside and the pilot showed Jay the radio. He pointed out how the radio helps a pilot when a plane is flying.

Jay pretended to be a real aviator and sat in the pilot's seat. When the day came to a close, Jay told his tale over and over to his mother and to his pals. He told them that when he was grown up, he was going to be a real pilot, and fly everywhere.

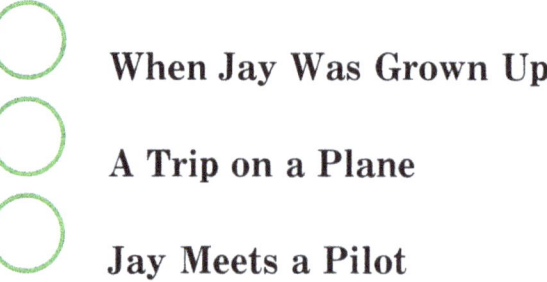

○ When Jay Was Grown Up

○ A Trip on a Plane

○ Jay Meets a Pilot

On the trip they slept in a ☐☐.

1. tent   2. tiny

The man had ☐ to the lady about driving ☐.

1. safely   2. spoken

You can ☐ a ☐ tomato on a table.

1. roll   2. ripe

The boat was not ☐, so they ☐ away.

1. sold   2. sailed

They tipped the box ☐ so that they could ☐ it.

1. open   2. over

Mother came ☐ from the food shop with the ☐

1. bacon   2. back

The ☐ lady gave the boy a ☐.

1. kind   2. kite

The snowman was ☐ melting in the ☐.

1. sunshine   2. slowly

Tony's leg was ☐, so he couldn't go to the ☐.

1. show   2. swollen

Father couldn't find his ☐ of ☐.

1. paint   2. pint

Kate Plans to Be an Aviator

One fine July evening Peter was helping Kate plan her life.

"What would you like to do when you're a grownup?" asked Peter.

"It's difficult to say," said Kate. "I find there are so many things I'd like to do! I'd like to have a stable where I'd be able to train my own pony. I'd like to visit Sweden. I'd like to make music and play with a traveling group. I'd like to tame lions."

"Wouldn't you like to be a wife and rock your baby in its cradle?" Peter asked.

"I wouldn't mind it," said Kate, "if I could still travel. I want to go where it's cold and slide in the snow. I want to see a tiger in the wild — not just in the zoo. The truth is, there are too many things to do. If I choose only one, would I have to forget the rest?"

"Maybe not," Peter told her. "I know — why not become an aviator? Then you could pilot your own plane to different lands. You could go to Sweden and Africa and even the South Pole. Is that the kind of life you'd like?"

"I think it is," Kate said. "I think I'll find out about becoming an aviator."

	Yes	No
1. Kate said that she wanted to fix auto radios when she got big.	○	○
2. Kate would enjoy making music with a group.	○	○
3. Kate wouldn't mind being a mother, if she could travel.	○	○
4. Peter told Kate she should become an alligator.	○	○
5. Kate would like to go where there's snow and meet an Eskimo.	○	○
6. Kate liked what Peter told her about an aviator's life.	○	○

My family lives in Sweden.

When I go outside in winter, it's very cold and snowy.

Sometimes it is below zero outside my home.

Am I — an alligator / a little boy / an elevator

Children like to make it out of snow.

It is ruined if the sun is too hot.

It doesn't mind the cold wind or the snow.

Is it — a rainbow / a shadow / a snowman

It is a wild animal.

It has black and yellow stripes.

You can visit it in the zoo if you're not afraid of its big teeth.

Is it — a title / a tiger / a trial

It is a bug.

It can't fly.

It spins webs and traps flies.

Is it — a spider / a child / a tiger

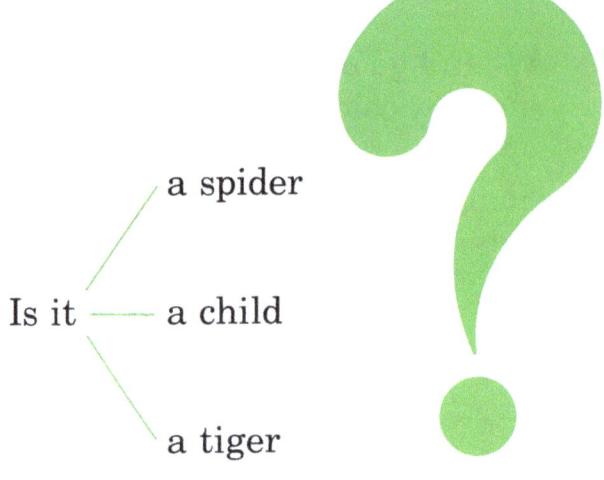

It is found inside, not outside.

It is like a little room.

You can ride up and down in it.

Is it — a radiator / an elevator / an aviator

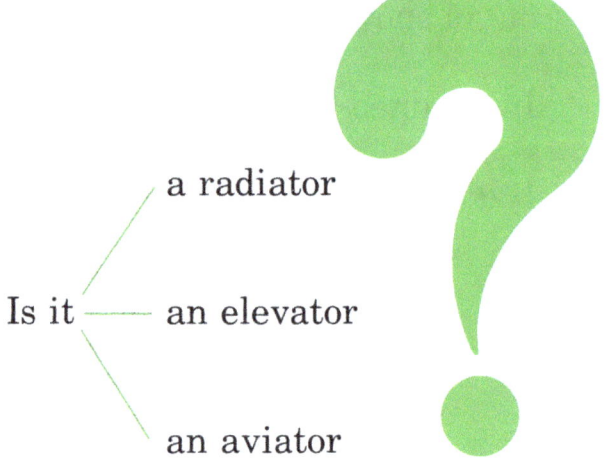

9

It is a valuable metal.

It is yellow.

Some rings are made of it.

Is it — a radio / a shadow / gold

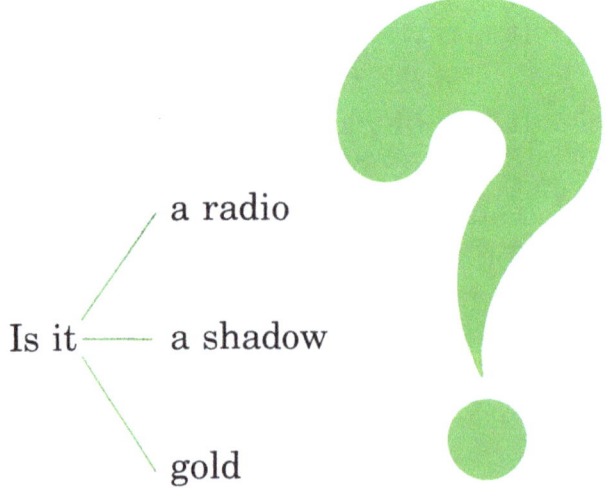

www.ingramcontent.com/pod-product-compliance
Lightning Source LLC
Chambersburg PA
CBHW081500070526
44586CB00019B/2444